PowerKids Readers:

My World™

My Bedtime
A Book About Getting Ready for Bed

Heather Feldman

The Rosen Publishing Group's
PowerKids Press™
New York

For Lauren and Ronnie Hochman and Jonathan Lowenberg—
the greatest siblings in the world.

Published in 2000 by The Rosen Publishing Group, Inc.
29 East 21st Street, New York, NY 10010

First Edition

Book design: Danielle Primiceri

Photo Illustrations by: Thaddeus Harden

Feldman, Heather L.
      My bedtime : a book about getting ready for bed / by Heather Feldman.
      p. cm. — (My world)
      Includes index.
      Summary: A little girl goes through various activities, including putting on her pajamas, brushing her teeth, reading a story, and being tucked in, as she gets ready to go to sleep.
      ISBN 0-8239-5522-2 (lib. bdg.)
      1. Bedtime—Juvenile literature. [1. Bedtime. 2. Night.] I. Title. II. Series: Feldman, Heather L.
My world.
HQ784.B43F45   1998
306.4—dc21

                                                    98-49480
                                                    CIP
                                                    AC

Manufactured in the United States of America

Contents

It is time for bed!
I put on my cozy pink
pajamas.

5

I put away my toys.

I brush my teeth.
I wash my face.
Scrub! Scrub!

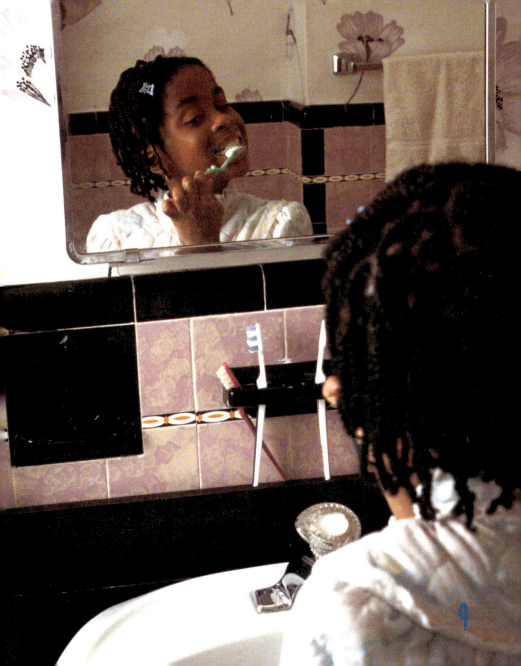

I fix my hair.

I find my teddy bear.

I read a storybook.

I get a good-night kiss.
I even get one more!

Now I am all tucked in
my bed.

Shhh! It is time for sweet
dreams.
Goodnight!

Words to Know

BED

PAJAMAS

PINK

TEDDY BEAR

TOYS

STORYBOOK

Here are more books to read about bedtime:
Say Good Night! Puffin Easy to Read, Level 1
by Harriet Ziefert, illustrated by Catherine
Siracusa
Puffin Books

Sleep Is for Everyone (Let's Read-And-Find-Out
Science)
by Paul Showers, illustrated by Wendy Watson
Harper Trophy

To learn more about getting ready for bed,
check out this Web site:
http://www.kidnaround.com/do.html

Index

Word Count: 67

Note to Parents, Teachers, and Librarians

PowerKids Readers are specially designed to get emergent and beginning readers excited about learning to read. Simple stories and concepts are paired with photographs of real kids in real-life situations. Spirited characters and story lines that kids can relate to help readers respond to written language by linking meaning with their own everyday experiences. Sentences are short and simple, employing a basic vocabulary of sight words, as well as new words that describe familiar things and places. Large type, clean design, and photographs corresponding directly to the text all help children to decipher meaning. Features such as a picture glossary and an index help children get the most out of PowerKids Readers. Lists of related books and Web sites encourage kids to explore other sources and to continue the process of learning. With their engaging stories and vivid photo-illustrations, PowerKids Readers inspire children with the interest and confidence to return to these books again and again. It is this rich and rewarding experience of success with language that gives children the opportunity to develop a love of reading and learning that they will carry with them throughout their lives.